WITHAM

KELVEDON, HATFIELD PEVEREL, SILVER END AND RIVENHALL

A Pictorial History

This copy engraving shows Newland Street, *c.*1825, looking towards Chelmsford. In those days Witham was an important stop-over for both stage and mail coaches.

WITHAM

KELVEDON, HATFIELD PEVEREL, SILVER END AND RIVENHALL

A Pictorial History

John Marriage

Phillimore

1995

Published by
PHILLIMORE & CO. LTD.,
Shopwyke Manor Barn, Chichester, West Sussex

ISBN 1 86077 000 2

Printed and bound in Great Britain by
BIDDLES LTD.
Guildford, Surrey

This book is dedicated to my no.3 grandson,
Phillip Marriage,
born whilst it was being prepared

List of Illustrations

Frontispiece: Newland Street, *c.*1825

Acknowledgements

In preparing this book I have received considerable help from a large number of people and organisations. I would especially like to thank Mr. Adam Smith of the Braintree Museum, Colchester and East Essex Co-operative Society Ltd., Crittall Windows plc, Mr. Carol De Coverley, Mr.and Mrs. Ibbotson and the Hon. G.R. Strutt, all of whom loaned me various items of memorabilia and provided me with valuable information. Finally, but not least, I must also thank my wife who cheerfully corrected grammatical and spelling errors and made many invaluable suggestions on the contents.

The author wishes to thank the following for permsission to reproduce photographs and illustrations: Mrs. M.G. Ager, 51; Mr. Eric Boesch, 29; Mr. Nigel Bowdidge, 89, 90, 91, 156; Braintree Museum, 2, 4-6, 9, 11, 12, 14, 15, 17, 26, 54, 58-61, 79-82, 86, 87, 111, 115, 116, 118, 120-2, 128, 130, 131, 143, 158-60, 162-4, 169; Mr. Bill Busby, 113; Clarkes of Chelmsford, 56, 57; Colchester and East Essex Cooperative Society, 42, 62-7, 168; Mr. Carol De Coverley, 35, 37, 53, 70, 72, 79, 80, 145-52, 166; Crittall Windows plc, 45-50, 83-5, 88, 110, 112, 133, 170; Essex County Police, 52, 119, 141-3; Essex Record Office, 36, 81, 100, 123, 139; Mr. Arthur H. Frost, 30, 31, 33, 34, 76, 78, 97, 109, 117, 124, 125, 144, 172; Mrs. Barbara Ibbotson, 3, 7, 13, 18-20, 23-25, 27, 28, 55, 137, 165; Mr. J.H. Meredith, 93-5; Mr. Alan Osborne, 102, 103, 105-8; Mrs. Pat A. Slugocki, 10, 22, 68, 104, 126, 127, 134, 136, 157; Lord Rayleigh's Dairies, 73-5, 77, 114, 129, 153, 154, 161, 167, 171.

All the remainder come from the author's own collection.

Introduction

Witham, together with Kelvedon, Hatfield Peverel and neighbouring communities, is almost in the very centre of Essex, surrounded by attractive undulating land, much in agricultural use but also containing scattered remnants of the forest of Essex. The district is drained by the river Blackwater and its tributary, the Brain, together with the Ter, which flows into the Chelmer, itself to unite with the Blackwater at Maldon. In former times all these rivers provided power for the water mills sited at regular intervals along them.

The original Witham settlement was at Chipping Hill, about half a mile to the north of the present town centre. Its origins go back more than 2,000 years, when an iron-age fort was built on the hill. In A.D. 912 a larger fort or 'burh' was constructed by King Edward, the elder of Alfred's sons, around these earlier works and eventually a permanent community, with a weekly market, became established between the burh and the river Brain.

Initially, Witham was part of a royal manor, but in 1147 Queen Matilda granted the manor to the Order of the Knights Templar and in 1215 they received permission from King John to hold an additional market for the purpose of trading with travellers, on the long established main London to Colchester road, in a place they called 'La Newe lande'.

Like Chelmsford and Braintree, both planned new towns, Newlands was marked out to a regular design with individual plots created in the form of long strips of land set at right angles to the road, with each strip curving down to the river. The town entrance from London was probably at the river Brain and a market cross was reputedly sited at the entrance to Lockram Lane. Development was set back alongside the road to allow a substantial trading area. Today, the wide part of Newland Street still follows the alignment established in those times.

Over the centuries the importance of the original settlement at Chipping Hill dwindled and its market discontinued but the Newland community prospered and eventually took over the title of 'Witham' from the Chipping Hill area. Today, the latter still retains its 'village-like' atmosphere.

Newland Street became an important stop-over for horse-drawn traffic between London, Colchester and Norwich, and four or five coaching inns catered for this trade. By 1834, just prior to the construction of the railways, there were 20 licensed stage coaches passing through Witham on what had become the Great Essex turnpike. Overnight accommodation and a change of horses were provided. Principal stopping places included *The Spread Eagle*, *The White Hart* and *Blue Post*. There was also considerable traffic along the Maldon to Braintree turnpike which passed through the town, crossing the main road at right angles. Frequent carrier services also went through, as well as animals 'on the hoof'. All these activities enhanced the town's prosperity. The market was held every Tuesday in the wide part of Newlands Street.

Witham for a time in the 18th century was a fashionable spa. Its spring waters in Faulkbourne Road attracted residents and visitors alike. One such visitor was Daniel Defoe, who was favourably impressed by the place. At this time many of the attractive buildings flanking Newlands Street were built or refronted.

Witham had a wide range of enterprises associated with its rôle as a market town. They included water mills for grinding corn, together with breweries and maltings. Coachbuilders and smithies also flourished. For a period, like nearby Braintree and Bocking, it was involved in the wool weaving trade. The town also had an important glove industry and more recently it has been associated with engineering. In the 1920s the well-known Braintree firm of Crittall's opened a branch factory. This became the town's major source of employment. The mid-20th century saw the growth of commuting between the various factories at Chelmsford, Braintree and Colchester and many Witham residents were employed in factories elsewhere. In 1846 Witham had a population of 3,500, but in 1952 the Urban District, which by then included Rivenhall and Silver End, had risen to 8,500 people.

Today, the town has a population of about 23,000 people. Crittall's has gone but instead there is a substantial industrial estate near the A12 bypass. Nevertheless, large numbers of people now commute each day to London by way of a frequent electric train service. However, Newlands Street still presents a pleasant, mainly Georgian appearance with many interesting old buildings flanking it, including *The Spread Eagle* and *The White Hart*. Another outstanding building is the present Town Hall, which has been one of the most important structures in the town for nearly 500 years. Once it was *The George* coaching inn but in about 1800 the inn closed and part of it reopened as the Witham Bank, the first bank in the town. It continued in this use until 1939 when it became occupied by several commercial users. In 1993 it was acquired by the Council and converted to its present civic use.

As a shopping centre, Witham currently faces considerable competition from the larger regional retail complexes at Chelmsford and Colchester. Nevertheless, small modern shopping precincts have appeared in the town. In earlier times many of the shops were locally owned by individual proprietors living above the shop or, if prosperous and successful, in villas nearby. Today most of the shops are branches of chain stores. The number of public houses, as in most communities, has declined.

Local entertainment, too, has suffered with the growth of car mobility; the Whitehall cinema, once a favourite meeting place for young and old, has succumbed to competition from television and multi-screen cinemas, as elsewhere. The cinema has an interesting history as it was originally a private house in the ownership of a Mr. Binden Blood. Some time before the Great War it became boys's school and in 1927 it was acquired as a cinema, a barn-like rear extension was added as the auditorium, and an Art Deco 'Odeon'-style cinema façade replaced the original house front. More recently the building has been converted into a library and the elegant façade has been restored.

1 This fascinating aerial photograph of Witham, *c.*1930, shows virtually the whole town straddling the old Roman Road, which runs straight as a die into the distance, towards Colchester.

High Street, Witham.

2 This view of Newland Street was taken at about the turn of the century, looking towards the Collingwood Road junction. The building with the projecting clock was the Constitutional Club which burnt to the ground in February 1910.

3 The same scene about 1915. A few off-duty soldiers can be seen lounging under the shop blinds. The club site remains empty, but the adjacent property has had a new flank wall built incorporating large sash windows.

4 Prior to the fire the Congregational Church (now United Reform) had been tucked away behind the club premises. Afterwards the club site was made into a garden, providing the church with a more natural setting. Today, it still remains open, although remodelled.

5 A view of Newland Street looking towards Bridge Street, busy with horse-drawn traffic and children. The Constitutional Club can be seen in the centre of the picture, *c.*1905.

6 Bridge Street, looking towards Hatfield Peverel at the turn of the century. The line of telephone poles indicates the coming advance in telecommunications.

7 Newland Street at its junction with Maldon Road, *c.*1950. The present shopping precinct was to appear a few years later.

8 Two of the best known public houses in the town are seen in this view of Newland Street, *c.*1950. In the foreground is the *Spread Eagle* whilst in the distance, past the junction with Maldon Road, is the *White Hart Hotel*.

9 *(left)*   The Newland Street/Collingwood Road junction was unusually quiet when this picture was taken, *c*.1905, and the policeman on point duty had little to do. The building then occupied by Glover Brothers has since been demolished and the site is now occupied by offices.

10 *(below left)*   Another well-known public house, the *Red Lion* is shown, *c*.1915, on the right-hand side of the picture, whilst opposite is the terrace house of Dorothy Sayers and beyond is the White Hall, then almost on the town's perimeter.

11 *(below)*   Roslyn House, *c*.1955, is a beautiful timber-framed building probably dating back to the 16th century and refronted in brick during the Georgian period. It provides an attractive stop to the top end of Newland Street.

The Environs

THE GROVE WITHAM. (FRONT VIEW)

12 'The Grove', pictured here *c.*1905, was a beautiful mansion standing in its own grounds towards the northern end of Newland Street. It was built in the late 17th century by Robert Barwell, a prosperous cloth merchant, and was enlarged in the 18th century by the Earl of Abercorn. In 1761, after landing at Harwich, Princess Charlotte stayed there on her way to be married to King George III. The house was demolished in 1932.

13 *(top right)* This side view of 'The Grove', *c.*1905, was taken from within the enclosing wall and shows part of the landscaped grounds.

14 *(bottom right)* The entrance hall to 'The Grove', *c.*1905, showing some of the heavily ornamental decor. The magnificent wooden staircase was reputedly taken from the original 17th-century building and reused when the house was remodelled in the 18th century.

15 The Avenue, *c*.1900, showing a distant view of 'The Grove'. The trees were planted by Earl Abercorn to provide a vista. The beautiful limes were felled when the house was demolished and the land was sold for development.

16 The Avenue, after development, *c*.1935.

17 These cottages with unusual mansard roofs, *c*.1905, in Newland Street accommodated employees of 'The Grove'.

18 & 19 Two views of Collingwood Road near its junction with Newland Street. Trees were planted rather unusually in the gutter, creating a hazard even in the days of light traffic. A lady driving a donkey cart was a rare sight even in 1905.

20 The Jubilee Oak, *c*.1930, at the junction of Collingwood Road and Guithavon Road, commemorates Queen Victoria's Jubilee. It was planted by Lady Luard, the wife of Admiral Sir William Luard, on 8 December 1887.

21 Colchester Road, *c.*1935, was a very quiet exit to the town.

22 In the 1930s and '40s the Aye-Aye Café on the London side of Witham was a welcome sight for the traveller. Today, the same property stands beside the A12 slip road and is now a garage selling cars and petrol.

THE AYE - AYE CAFÉ
WITHAM, ESSEX.
ON MAIN LONDON—COLCHESTER—EAST COAST ROAD
'PHONE:- WITHAM 133.   (E. J. HARTWELL-JONES)

23 All Saints' Church in Guithavon Street, *c.*1905, was built in 1842 by J. Brown of Norwich as a chapel of ease for St Nicholas parish church, Chipping Hill. However, in 1969, it became redundant and closed. It was reopened in 1989 as the Holy Family & All Saints' RC Church.

Guithavon Road, Witham

Copyright WTHM.

24 Chipping Hill, *c.*1910. On the right is the village smithy. All eyes are turned to watch the photographer. The children are probably from the nearby Barnardiston House, then a private school.

25 Chipping Hill is the site of the original Witham settlement. Although surrounded by more recent development, it still retains its village atmosphere, as this *c.*1910 view across the green shows.

26 Church Street, Chipping Hill, *c.*1900, was then a very quiet highway and disturbed by little more than the occasional horse and cart. Until 1839 the terrace in the centre of the picture was the parish workhouse.

27 A pretty view of St Nicholas' Church, Chipping Hill, seen from across the river Brain, *c*.1910.

28 Typical Edwardian dwellings in Braintree Road, *c.*1910. They are substantially brick-built with slate roofs and provide solid, if austere, comfort.

29 This picture of Blue Mills on the river Blackwater is framed by the road arch and was taken by a passing canoeist about 1950. Once a prosperous watermill, it is now a private house.

The District

Kelvedon

Kelvedon is a linear village along the old Roman road from London to Colchester and once had its own market. It is reputedly the site of the Roman settlement of Canonium, and excavations reveal that a Belgic tribe was settled in the vicinity before the Roman occupation. For many years the village suffered from heavy through traffic but now some degree of peace has returned following the construction of the A12 bypass. There is a wealth of interesting buildings, many of great age, along its length and fortunately the village has been little spoilt by modern development. The bridge over the Blackwater is effectively the dividing line between Kelvedon and the adjoining village of Feering, although nowadays the two communities merge together. However, the original village of Feering was on the road leading to Coggeshall.

In the last century the area became well known for horticulture and it was here that the Kelvedon Wonder strain of seeds originated. The area was also well known for the production of lavender. Today, the area still supports seed trial grounds run by the firm of Kings Seed growers.

The village was the birthplace of the Baptist preacher, Charles Haddon Spurgeon (1834-92), in a small white cottage in the High Street. He preached at the vast Metropolitan Tabernacle in London from 1861; it was destroyed by fire in 1989.

Although Kelvedon still boasts a variety of shops which serve local needs, at the turn of the century it was an almost totally self-contained community and enjoyed a much wider variety of stores, where villagers could purchase virtually all their day-to-day needs. As well as chemists, tailors, drapers and grocers there were other trades, long gone, like clothiers, hatters and coopers.

Hatfield Peverel

The original village is situated along the old Roman road, later the Essex Great Road, between Chelmsford and Colchester. A Benedictine priory, a cell of St Albans Abbey, was once located on the edge of the village. The present large parish church, dedicated to St Andrew, is the nave of the former priory church to which has been added a 15th-century aisle and another built in 1873. However, the chancel and most of the remainder of the priory have disappeared, apart from a few wall stumps.

Although the village grew up around the junction of the Essex Great Road, with a route to Maldon, newer development has taken place mainly to the south, much of it in post-war years, particularly following the construction of the present A12 bypass. In 1801 the village had a population of 1,008, in 1951 it was 2,175 and today there are about 4,000 people. Most now commute to London or other urban areas. Like Kelvedon, the range of shops serving the village has steadily reduced throughout the century both in overall numbers and variety as people turn to the large shopping centres like Chelmsford and Colchester for their needs and there is now little community focus. Although the village once supported a substantial brewery, today the largest industrial activity is a milk bottling plant.

Silver End

Silver End was built as a planned garden village by Crittall's, the Braintree-based engineering firm. In the early 1920s the firm was rapidly expanding and the local council began to have difficulty in providing homes for the employees and the firm decided to build their own. Francis Henry Crittall, after rejecting ideas of building a substantial housing estate in or around Braintree, decided that it would be preferable to build a completely new garden village on a virgin site, where each householder could have a garden and where communal services could be provided. In this he followed many of the ideas of Ebenezer Howard, the founder of the Garden City Movement and an early member of the present Royal Town Planning Institute. He was also influenced by the development of Bournville by George Cadbury and Saltaire by Sir Titus Salt.

In November 1925, a farm called Boars Tye Farm at Silver End, then within a remote agricultural area, was acquired. Enough land was purchased to provide homes for some 7,500 people. They were built to the remarkably low density of six houses to the acre, and each had a substantial garden area which the tenants could enjoy. Each house had hot and cold running water, the former being a rarity in those days. The village was designed to be completely self-sufficient with its own water supply and drainage—with churches, hotel, cinema, a departmental shop and bus services, as well as having generous recreational open space. The layout provided tree-lined avenues radiating from the centre and gardens at street junctions. In addition, a mixed farm of 264 acres was purchased to produce fresh food, including meat and vegetables. This was sold through the departmental store directly to the villagers. Also included within the development was a 'fittings' factory, especially constructed to enable disabled men to carry on working. This was, for the times, a far-sighted idea, but very welcome in view of the number of disabled ex-servicemen from the Great War.

Crittall's set up a special subsidiary, the Silver End Development Company, to build the village and among the directors was Captain Reiss who was also on the board of the much larger and better known Welwyn Garden City, in Hertfordshire. He appointed Murrey Hennell to prepare the layout of the village, and he also designed many of the houses and other buildings. Others were designed by C.H.B. Quennell and Thomas Tait of Sir John Burnet and Partners, who were awarded the best 'house of the year' design in the 1928 Ideal Home Exhibition for two managers houses built in the village. The general appearance of the village is considered to be one of the earliest instances in the county of the style known as 'Modern', many being built with flat roofs and distinctive metal windows. Concurrently with the construction of the first houses, the factory began to function. Its power plant provided unlimited electricity for the residents. Soon schools, shops and churches followed and in 1927 the newly-built school had a full roll of 135 pupils. In 1927, Francis Crittall and his wife moved into the village at 'The Manors' and it remained his home until his death in 1934.

When the Crittall Company was taken over by Slater, Walker Securities in 1968, the houses were acquired by Witham Urban District Council; today many are privately owned and the village has been designated a Conservation Area. In post-war years further residential development has been built around the original community, to a standard suburban style destroying some of its architectural integrity.

Rivenhall

Rivenhall is still a rural village. Like Kelvedon there are reputed to be Roman remains. During the war years a military airfield was constructed within the parish, occupied for some time by the United States Army Air Force. From this airfield Marauders—a type of fast fighter bomber—took part in many sorties over occupied Europe and Nazi Germany. After its liberation they moved to France and the airfield then became the home of RAF Horsa gliders, who took part in the tragic Arnhem offensive. In the early post-war years the airmen's huts were taken over temporarily by Polish refugees until permanent accommodation was provided elsewhere.

Wickham Bishops

Wickham Bishops is a well-wooded area set in undulating land to the south west of Witham, from which it is now separated by the A12 Witham bypass as well as the river Blackwater. Although not within the parish, Blue Mills provides a pleasant setting, though no longer working. Further downstream stood Wickham Mill. At the height of its importance, in about 1880, it had a steam engine to supplement the water power. It was demolished in 1975 but the former mill house, Wickham Place, survives. Philip Morant, the well-known Essex historian, who has the honour of having a street named after him in Colchester, was the rector of St Bartholomew's Church from 1742-5; the church is now a ruin. The present church is a prominent landmark as it stands on the top of the hill and is close to modern development. To the north of Wickham Bishops are Great and Little Braxted, two more rural parishes. Within the Little Braxted parish is another attractive mill, the most striking feature of which is the fact that the public road passes immediately below its walls. Nearby is the attractive Braxted Park which is unusual in Essex through being surrounded by a five-feet high brick wall, with a total perimeter of 4½ miles. Braxted Park House is the centrepiece of this beautiful estate and stands beside an attractive landscaped lake.

Kelvedon and Feering

30 The London entrance to Kelvedon is via St Mary's Square where the village market, now discontinued, was once held. Although most of the buildings seen in this picture, *c*.1862, still remain, the square is now little more than a double bend in the main road.

31 Kelvedon High Street as seen from St Mary's Square at the turn of the century, showing a wealth of attractive old houses.

32 The High Street, *c*.1930, before cars dominated the scene and when the main drama was the hourly bus to Chelmsford or Colchester. On the left is C.H. Spurgeon's birthplace.

33 Once a huge variety of shops served the local community. Here, *c*.1865, a signwriter is carefully applying lettering to the fascia of J. Osborne's shop. He was a highly regarded shoemaker. From the workroom above, several of his men can be seen watching the photographer.

34 The *Swan Inn*, next to the new bridge, *c*.1862, was an important commercial and posting inn and was advertised as having 'good stabling, large yards, compact brewhouse and other conveniences'. In the distance, down Swan Lane, is Easterford Mill.

35 A view of the river Blackwater, *c.*1900, looking towards Ewell Hall and Kelvedon.

Remains of Old Coach Road

36 *(above)* This panoramic 1920s sketch shows the remains of the old coach road, the medieval bridge and the site of the ford which linked Kelvedon with the adjoining village of Feering. After the construction of the new bridge the route fell into disuse.

37 *(left)* The *Sun Inn*, Feering, with the new bridge, *c.*1900. In the distance, on the far side of the river Blackwater, Kelvedon High Street can be seen.

38 *(right)* The railway bridge over the Blackwater, upstream from the new bridge, *c.*1920. In those days a covered passage leading from the main-line railway station to the lower station was attached to the bridge structure. The lower station served the Tollesbury Line.

Kelvedon.
R. Blackwater
from Bridge

C. J. STANILAND

Hatfield Peverel and Terling

39 This attractive pair of houses was situated on the Chelmsford side of Hatfield Peverel near the river Ter. In the distance is the village mill.

40 Hatfield Peverel Mill was a five-storey structure built about 1790. Unusually, it had both an overshot wheel and a breast shot wheel for grinding the corn. The mill was built directly facing the road with its pond on the far side. It was demolished in 1931. This picture was taken by Fred Spalding, the well-known Chelmsford photographer, at about the turn of the century.

41 In post-war days Hatfield Peverel has seen a considerable amount of commuter development. However, this merely continued a trend which started in the 1930s, as this picture of Station Road confirms.

42 The original Witham Co-operative Society branch shop at The Green is pictured here, *c.*1930. In 1932 it was replaced by a substantial purpose-built store.

43 Terling Place was built by John Strutt in 1772 and remains occupied by his descendants. In the foreground and separated from the grounds of the house by a ha-ha are cattle owned by Lord Rayleigh's Dairies, *c.*1900.

44 This beautiful country scene at Church Green, Terling was captured by Fred Spalding, *c*.1905. The timbered house was once the offices for Lord Rayleigh's estate.

Silver End

45 An aerial view of Silver End Garden Village still under construction in 1928.

46 Although there were several individual designs, houses were built using mass production methods adapted from those in Crittall's factories. Here, some of the pitched roofed houses are under construction, *c.*1928.

47 Most of the new houses at Silver End were semi-detached but two magnificent houses were built for managers. They were designed by Mr. T.S. Tait of Sir John Burnet Parners, who was awarded the 'best house design' award of the year at the Ideal Home Exhibition in 1928.

48 & 49 The *Silver End Hotel* and the Village Hall. Although the village provided good housing and working conditions, the younger inhabitants complained that there was little to do in the evenings other than to visit the hotel or the hall, even though the latter was the venue for much varied entertainment.

50 'The Manors' was built as a dominant contribution to the village, located on an axis with the Village Hall and looking across the Memorial Gardens. Francis Crittall lived here from the time it was built in 1927 until he died in 1934. It was designed by C.H.B. Quennell.

Rivenhall

51 In 1932 Rivenhall End was just a quiet group of cottages strung along the main London to Colchester road. The terrace with the dormer windows was known as the Workhouse Cottages. Today, the same road is a busy dual carriageway and the cottages have gone.

52 *(top right)* The life of a rural policeman was mostly uneventful and at Rivenhall police station, *c.*1920, there were few crimes to contend with.

53 *(bottom right)* This was the idyllic scene in Rickstones Road, Rivenhall, *c.*1920.

Commerce

54 The Witham Town Hall (right of picture) occupies one of the town's most historic sites. As *The George Inn* its origins go back nearly 500 years. In 1880 the inn closed and the building was remodelled and converted into the Witham Bank. In course of time it became a branch of Barclays Bank, and in the 1990s it became the Town Hall.

55 *The Spread Eagle Hotel*, in Newland Street, *c.*1915 was one of the town's principal coaching inns, dating back to medieval times. It remains of considerable importance in the social life of the community. In Victorian times the covering plasterwork was removed to expose the underlying timber beams.

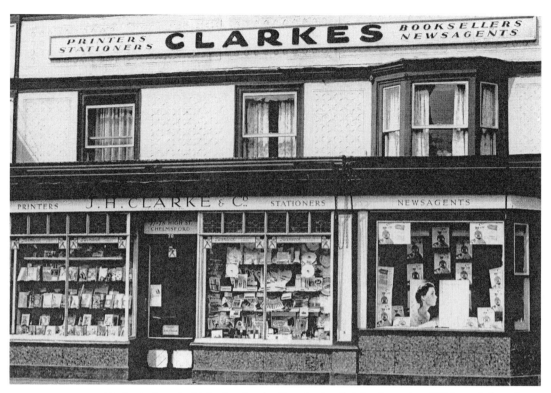

56 In the 1950s Clarke & Co., the high class booksellers, had a thriving branch at Witham. It has since closed. Their main premises are at Chelmsford.

57 An important part of Clarke's business was the sale of office equipment. This extract from a stock brochure, *c.*1950, shows a selection of some of their latest typewriters.

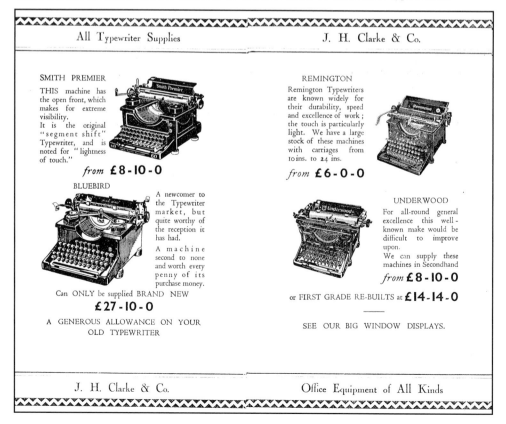

All Typewriter Supplies   J. H. Clarke & Co.

SMITH PREMIER

THIS machine has the open front, which makes for extreme visibility.
It is the original "segment shift" Typewriter, and is noted for "lightness of touch."

from **£8-10-0**

REMINGTON

Remington Typewriters are known widely for their durability, speed and excellence of work; the touch is particularly light. We have a large stock of these machines with carriages from 10 ins. to 24 ins.

from **£6-0-0**

BLUEBIRD

A newcomer to the Typewriter market, but quite worthy of the reception it has had.
A machine second to none and worth every penny of its purchase money.

Can ONLY be supplied BRAND NEW
£27-10-0

A GENEROUS ALLOWANCE ON YOUR OLD TYPEWRITER

UNDERWOOD

For all-round general excellence this well-known make would be difficult to improve upon.
We can supply these machines in Secondhand

from **£8-10-0**

or FIRST GRADE RE-BUILTS at **£14-14-0**

SEE OUR BIG WINDOW DISPLAYS.

J. H. Clarke & Co.   Office Equipment of All Kinds

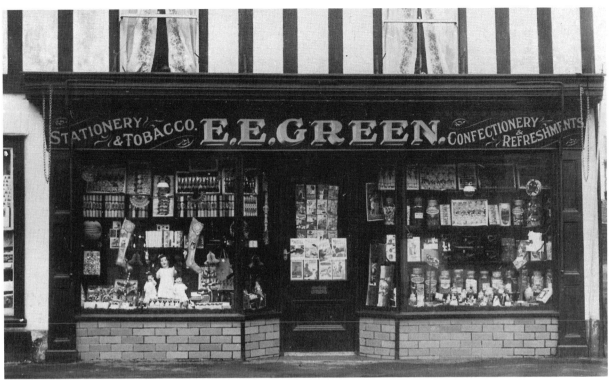

58 Well before the days of supermarkets and chain stores, shopkeepers owned their own stores and lived above them. A typical case was that of Miss Emma Ethel Green who had a shop at 26 High Street, *c.*1920.

59 One of the most interesting shop fronts in Witham, *c.*1925, was at 37 Newland Street which consisted of twin Georgian bay windows. This building of character has long since gone.

60 In 1897 Joseph Glover's cycle shop in Newland Street was a popular meeting place for cycling enthusiasts. In those times cycling was an essential form of transport for ordinary people as well as a cheap and new way of enjoying the countryside.

61 Glover's later moved to larger premises on the corner of Collingwood Road and the business gradually established itself as a motor garage, later moving to other premises.

62 The Witham Co-operative Society's well patronised premises in Newland Street in 1907. A particular feature was the elegant lamps over the windows. Sadly, the 20th century has not been kind to the movement and in 1970 the Witham Society was taken over by the Colchester and East Essex Society.

63, 64 & 65 In pre-war days the Witham and Maldon Co-operative Societies competed annually for the best shop window display. Two of the best Witham entries for 1931, together with one for 1935, are shown here. Whilst some of the products are still familiar, the prices are now totally beyond recognition.

66 The interior of the Witham Co-operative Society hardware store in Newland Street, c.1930, shows a variety of everyday household items of the times.

67 The centrepiece of Witham Co-operative Society's grocery and provisions shop, c.1935, was the hanging display of bacon joints—a practice which the hygiene regulations of today would certainly not permit.

CUSTOMERS WAITED ON DAILY

Best Home-Killed Meat

Spiced Beef

Pickled Tongues

JAMES SORRELL

FAMILY BUTCHER.   WITHAM

SAUSAGES, LARD, ETC.

TELEPHONE WITHAM 30

NO ORDER TOO LARGE, NONE TOO SMALL.

68 In 1932 James Sorrell ran a family business in Witham, supplying home-slaughtered meat to his customers and giving a very specialised service.

Industry

Being substantially agricultural, Witham and district is not an area which has attracted major manufacturing industries. In the past there have been traditional local enterprises dependent on agriculture, like maltings, tanneries and breweries. Indeed, in the last century one of the largest tanneries in the country operated at Witham in Mill Lane. The wool industry was represented there, although of less importance than at nearby Braintree and Bocking. The town was also noted for the manufacture of gloves. From small beginnings, by 1948, Pinkham's were producing about 4,000 pairs of gloves a week, employing some 300 workers.

In the early part of the century, The Crittall Manufacturing Company Ltd., a Braintree-based engineering firm, were rapidly expanding as a manufacturer of metal window frames and other forms of metal work. They decided to build a new factory in Braintree road, Witham, covering an area of some 11 acres. Their initial purpose was to make steel furniture, previously undertaken in their works at Braintree. In 1920 this business was taken over by Sankey Sheldon and the factory then concentrated on the manufacture of standard metal windows on mass production lines. In 1923, a further factory adjacent to the main plant opened to make standard skylights and, uniquely at the time, it was staffed entirely by women. Both these factories made a big contribution to the war effort 1939-45. They are now closed, and Crittall's are concentrated entirely in a new factory at Braintree. The former Crittall site at Braintree Road is occupied by Safeways superstore with 50,000 square feet of retail space. Its design reflects the 'modern movement' architecture of the former factory.

Hand in hand with the development of Silver End as a garden village, an integral part of the community, Crittall's also built a new factory, providing local employment as well as sufficient energy to give heat, light and pumped water to the village. Much of this factory had automatic or semi-automatic machinery and so the company was able to employ disabled personnel, particularly ex-servicemen from the Great War.

Today, the main industrial activity is concentrated on the large industrial estate on the north-east side of Witham. One of the factories is operated by Marconi-GEC for the manufacture of electronic equipment, in association with their factories at Chelmsford. Other firms in Witham are the Bush, Boake, Allen chemical plant and the maltsters, Hugh Bairds.

Agriculture remains of considerable importance in the district and one of the most successful enterprises is that of Lord Rayleigh's Farms. It is based on an estate approximately four miles in diameter, centred on the village of Terling and extending to both Hatfield Peverel and Witham. The land was originally acquired some 300 years ago from profits generated by the Strutt family's successful milling business in Chelmsford and Maldon. However, in the 1880s many of the tenant farmers on its 8,000 acres were made bankrupt by the great agricultural depression and so the Strutt family decided to farm the land directly. A farming partnership was set up by the 3rd Lord Rayleigh—a Nobel prize winning scientist—with his brother, Edward Strutt, who managed the enterprise. In addition to mixed farming, the policy was to introduce milk production, with London as its main market. This was highly successful. It was from these beginnings that the present Lord Rayleigh's Dairies have developed, supplying milk to supermarkets and many other outlets, including doorstep delivery. The milk is distributed from the Central Dairy at Hatfield Peverel. As a family concern, Lord Rayleigh's Farms Inc. have a policy of maintaining the quality of the environment and, whilst farming as efficiently as possible, they take great store in retaining and enhancing the natural habitat wherever possible. It is for this reason that their land retains a traditional landscape, with small fields bisected by hedgerows and trees, so typical of Essex. This is in marked contrast to that of many neighbouring farms, which in recent years have adopted the principle of creating huge hedgeless fields, with the result that some localities now have an open featureless 'prairie' landscape.

69 In the days of horse-drawn transport the blacksmith was a busy and important person in the life of the community. Here at the Chipping Hill Smithy, *c*.1938, he attends to two well cared for farm horses.

70 Feering Post Mill, Mill Lane, *c.*1900, played an important part in the economy of the village, grinding wheat into flour. Gradually large mechanical mills took over and windmills became redundant.

71 Cutting and baling wheat near Witham, *c.*1920. The bales were stacked in the field to dry in the sun and were then carted away for threshing.

72 Steam power was used at the turn of the century to thresh cereals. Here, the firm of Partridge of Coggeshall are threshing oats on a farm at Kelvedon. Today, diesel-powered combines do the job.

73 & 74 Potatoes have traditionally been stored against frost in straw-covered clamps until required for sale. These pictures, *c.*1950, show them being removed, sorted and bagged ready for sale.

75 Lord Rayleigh's Dairies were the very first producers to abandon the use of glass bottles. In 1960 they adopted triangular-shaped tetrapak cartons at their Hatfield Peverel bottling plant, mainly for use in shops and supermarkets. Today, other types are in vogue.

76 Down on the farm at the turn of the century, steam was used in a variety of ways. Here, a Darby patent plough from Wickford is at work preparing the soil for sowing.

77 More recently tractors have replaced both the steam plough and the traditional horse-drawn plough. In the late 1950s Lord Rayleigh's farms were using this huge caterpillar tractor.

78 Steam power was also found in the workshop and at a Kelvedon timber yard, *c.*1900, used to provide power to a massive circular saw, via belt drive.

79 The river Blackwater and its tributaries have been used to provide power for hundreds of years, with watermills regularly spaced along them. The mill at Kelvedon is pictured here at the turn of the century, when still used for grinding corn into flour.

80 With the development of steam power and the invention of roller milling, watermills began to be converted or replaced. In 1849 the Roller Flour Mill was constructed in Guithavon Road, near to an older watermill, in the traditional style, complete with lucum. In 1888 both plants were operated by E.M. Blyth. They ceased to work in 1925 and were later demolished. In 1932 a chapel was built on the site of the roller mill.

81 Another view of the same mill also showing the house and, on the far right, the original watermill. In the foreground, a beehive of traditional design can be seen. The land associated with the business extended to some 20 acres.

83 An aerial view of the Witham factory of the Crittall Manufacturing Company, *c.*1959. Although established in the 1920s, much of it was built in the 1930s. From 1939 to 1945 it went over to war work. In the early 1990s it was demolished and the site is currently occupied by a large superstore.

84 This aerial picture clearly shows the Crittall plant at Silver End, *c.*1959. It was built in the 1930s by the company as part of the concept of creating a self-

82 At the turn of the century the wheelwright was an important member of the community, making and repairing a wide range of horse-drawn vehicles. Robert Fleuty's busy workshop was situated in Howbridge Road.

contained new community in garden surroundings, an idea which was later to be developed elsewhere in Essex in the New Towns of Harlow and Basildon.

85 Crittall's made considerable use of mass production methods and this picture shows the final assembly of standard metal windows at the Witham plant, *c.*1950.

86 & 87 Crittall's used the railway for the delivery of a high proportion of their products. The window frames were boxed and craned into railway wagons from their own siding at Witham, *c*.1948.

88 Crittall's advertising in the 1920s was both novel and eye-catching. Models were built on trailers and went to fêtes, carnivals and exhibitions, displaying examples of their products.

Transport

The old Roman road from London to Colchester and Norwich has always been an important route for travellers and after the Romans departed it eventually became the Essex Great Road, a busy turnpike attracting many forms of traffic, including mail and stage coaches, private carriages and gigs. Local produce was brought to market by cart wagon or 'on the hoof'. Both Braintree and Witham received considerable quantities of raw material and merchandise shipped through the then important port of Maldon, with cumbersome vehicles negotiating a secondary turnpike connecting the three towns. However, in the middle of the 19th century much of this trade transferred to a new means of transport—the railway.

On 4 July 1836 the construction was authorised of the Eastern Counties Railway, to run from Bishopsgate, London to Colchester. Work started the following year and by 1843 a double track had been laid, passing through Hatfield Peverel, Witham and Kelvedon, with stations at all three places. Initially, the tracks were laid to a wide gauge of 5 feet but were converted to the present standard gauge of 4 feet 8½ inches between 5 September and 7 October 1844. The first passenger train to traverse the entire line puffed slowly along the route in March 1843. The Eastern Counties Railway was later absorbed by the Great Eastern Railway, and the track was to become the main East Coast line from London to Norwich and the various East Anglian ports. Following further amalgamations, it eventually became part of the London and Northern Eastern Railway, until post-war nationalisation, when it became part of the Eastern Region of British Railways.

As much of Braintree's and Witham's trade went through Maldon it is somewhat surprising that, like the neighbouring river Chelmer to Chelmsford, the river Blackwater was not made navigable. This would have permitted barges to deliver goods between Maldon and both the towns direct. However, no such steps were apparently ever taken and in 1845 plans were deposited with the local Clerk of the Peace for the construction of a 12-mile railway from Braintree, passing through Witham to Maldon, where, as part of the project, it was intended to construct a new ship dock to cater for an expected increase in coastal shipping. In June 1846 Royal Assent was given to an Act of Parliament for the construction of the railway to carry goods and materials between Maldon and both Witham and Braintree. The terminus of the new railway was at Braintree, with an elaborate station at Maldon. In addition, there were stations at Cressing, White Notley and Wickham Bishops and Langford. The main contractor was Thomas Jackson. At first, ownership was in the hands of its promoters, the Maldon, Witham and Braintree Railway Company, but it was soon acquired by the Eastern Counties Railway. The entire route had a double track and was opened with great ceremony on 2 October 1848. It soon became clear, however, that a single track would suffice and accordingly, during the Crimean War, one track was lifted and sold to the

War Department. Although the line was planned to cross the main line at Witham, in the event it was constructed as two branches, both running out of Witham station thereby discouraging through traffic. Both branches were completely integrated with the main line and the station consisted of two island platforms with the station offices on the overbridge. Main-line trains used the inner platform faces and the branches used the outer faces. Although started, the planned dock at Maldon was never completed and for many years cargo destined for Witham and Braintree was barged up the Chelmer & Blackwater Navigation to a point where the new railway crossed the canal near Maldon. Here, a special wharf and siding were built to allow the transfer of goods. The six-mile Maldon line continued to be used by traffic well into the second half of the present century but closed on 7 September 1964. Substantial traces of the line still remain, including a bridge under the present A12 Witham bypass. However, the six-mile Braintree branch survives and, like the main line, has been electrified, with Witham continuing to be its junction. Today, both Braintree and Witham offer a frequent electric service to London.

In 1903, the Great Eastern Railway Company constructed the Kelvedon and Tollesbury Light Railway with the aid of a Treasury grant of £16,000—one third of the estimated cost—with the intention of tapping developing interest in the Blackwater as a holiday and boating resort. The line started at Kelvedon and terminated at Tollesbury Pier on the Blackwater estuary—a total distance of 9¾ miles. Construction began at the Kelvedon end with the contractor employing over 200 men on the project. At Kelvedon the station was built at a lower level than the main-line station and trains ran a shuttle service along the line. A ramp provided a connection for goods traffic. Passenger trains on this line consisted of quaint little carriages, with open verandas at either end, from which travellers could view the countryside as the train puffed slowly along. Although busy for a time, trade—mainly of an agricultural nature—never came up to expectation and the line was cut back to Tollesbury Town station in 1921; it reopened briefly during the last war to carry arms and ammunition to shore batteries stationed around Tollesbury Wick Marshes. A particular traffic until the line was finally closed was to Wilkins Jam factory at Tiptree. Passenger services were withdrawn in 1950 and the whole line was closed from October 1962.

Between the wars coach and bus services were developed throughout the area. The largest company, now known as the Eastern National, was established in the early years of the century as the National Steam Car Company Ltd. in Chelmsford, using steam driven buses designed by Thomas Clarkson. Although most of their routes fanned out to the villages around Chelmsford, the company were soon running their steam buses along the old Roman road to and from Colchester. In doing so they were in competition with similar buses owned by Moores Brothers Ltd. of Kelvedon. The latter was a long established carrier business founded in 1815 by W.E. Moore with three donkeys and a cart. In 1881 the firm was running horse-drawn buses but other vehicles were acquired shortly afterwards. Later, the firm, by then consisting of three brothers also developed services to Braintree, Maldon and Coggeshall. Both the National and Moores soon turned to petrol-driven buses and competed fiercely on the profitable Chelmsford to Colchester service. Although the larger Eastern National used a variety of buses, Moores began to concentrate on Guy 'Arabs'. Another company operating in the area was the Braintree-based Hickes Bros. Ltd., who ran a regular service between Witham and Braintree as well as other services radiating from Braintree.

In 1950, Hickes Bros. was purchased by the British Transport Commission, who incorporated the business into that of the Eastern National. This was a fate also suffered by Moores Bros. Ltd. in 1963. Today, the main bus company operating throughout the area is the Eastern National Bus Company Ltd., although a smaller and relatively dynamic company, the Hedingham & District Omnibus Company Ltd., has established itself on a number of routes following its takeover in 1960 of the former Letch Bus Service of Sible Hedingham.

Rail

89 A steam train enters Witham station from Colchester direction, *c.*1925, passing the old maltings.

90 & 91 Before the First World War, Hatfield Peverel station still had a rural appearance, and a journey to London had to be well planned in advance. For the journey, a well-stocked bookstall, sited in the main buildings, was an important amenity.

92 Early this century railways were the premier means of travel. In addition to the main-line network there was a series of radiating light railways. One such track was the Tollesbury Line. It ran from Kelvedon Lower station, where it had a main-line connection, to the Blackwater Estuary. The Tollesbury train is seen here at the Lower station on 12 August 1950.

93 Along the line there were passenger halts. Most had a short platform and a crude shelter. At Feering, *c.*1950, an old horse bus had been pressed into service for this purpose.

94 & 95 The Tollesbury Line carriages were of a most unusual design. The interior consisted of a single compartment with bench seats on either side. At each end there were open verandahs, from which passengers could view the countryside as the train puffed slowly along the track. Photographed on 12 August 1950.

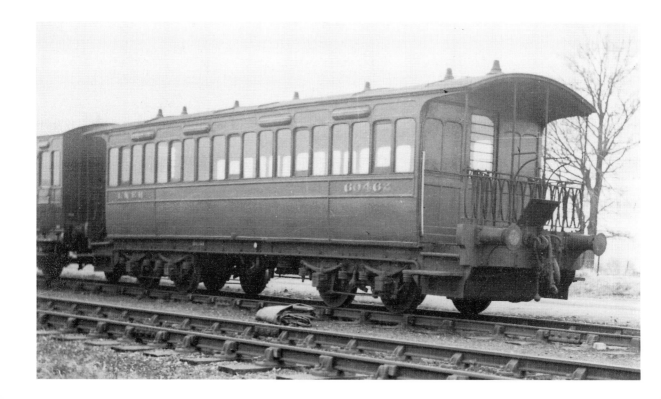

96 At the outbreak of the Second World War rail transport was already diminishing. Nevertheless, throughout the period of hostilities railways played a pivotal rôle in the movement of men and supplies.

Road

97 Ben Revett, landlord of the *Star & Fleece* public house, Kelvedon, is seen here, with a friend, driving his horse and trap through the village, *c.*1880.

98 The development of the bicycle in the last century enabled the working classes to have, for the first time, a degree of mobility. Cycling reached its peak in the 1940s and '50s. Here a lone cyclist pauses on the bridge at Dairy Hill, Terling, *c*.1900.

99 This farm cart was pictured crossing Hinds Brook Bridge, Worlds End Lane, Kelvedon, *c*.1900. The ubiquitous tractor came along in the 1950s, making the working horse redundant.

100 Waggons drawn by strong carthorses carried substantial loads for considerable distances. In 1914 army units stationed in Witham used them extensively.

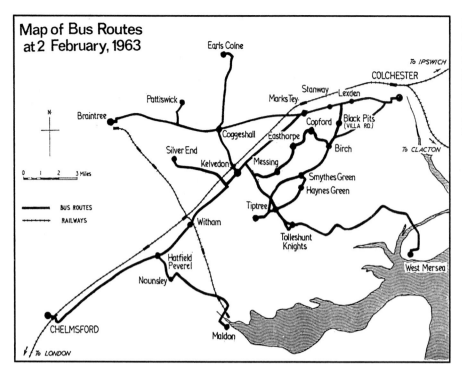

Map of Bus Routes at 2 February, 1963

Earls Colne
To IPSWICH
COLCHESTER
Pattiswick
Stanway Lexden
Marks Tey
Braintree
Copford
Black Pits (VILLA RD.)
Coggeshall
Easthorpe
To CLACTON
Silver End
Birch
Kelvedon
Messing
Smythes Green
Haynes Green
Tiptree
Witham
Tolleshunt Knights
West Mersea
Hatfield Peverel
Nounsley
CHELMSFORD
Maldon
To LONDON

N

0 1 2 3 Miles

BUS ROUTES
RAILWAYS

101 From the early part of the century Moores Brothers operated a successful bus company with services radiating from their garage at Kelvedon until it was taken over the Eastern National Bus Company in 1962. This diagram shows their routes at the time of takeover.

102 Originally, Moores ran a general carrier business from which the bus service developed. In this picture, dated about the turn of the century, their cart has at least one passenger in addition to goods on board.

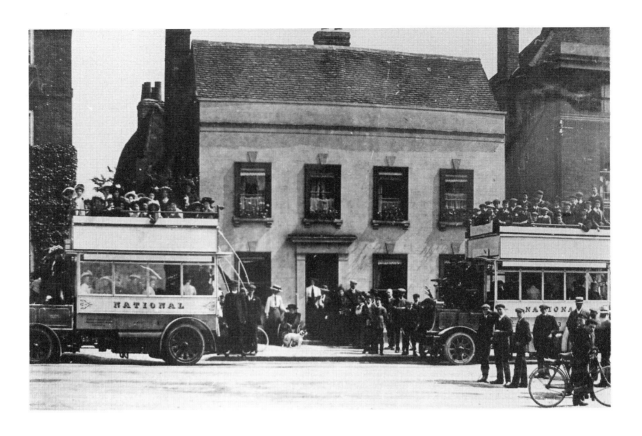

103 & 104 Moores purchased several steam buses from the National Company with whom they competed. However, by the 1920s, both were using motor buses on their routes between Chelmsford, Witham and Colchester.

105 Although many of Moores' buses were double-deckers, on some routes they had to use single-deckers due to low bridges. In the late 1920s, this Leyland Lion was a reliable member of their fleet.

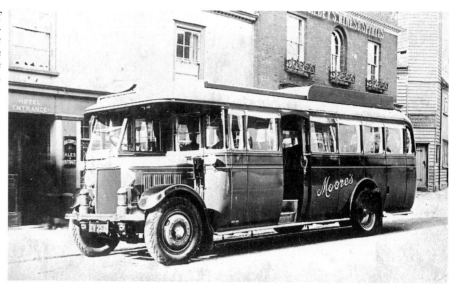

106 Moores also did contract work. One of their most important assignments was to take the Colchester United football team in a special coach to away fixtures, *c*.1955.

107 After the Eastern National took over Moores, their buses were repainted with the latter's livery. Here, one of Moores' former buses is seen at the Kelvedon Garage, *c*.1962.

108 Another operator in the district was Hicks Bros of Braintree. Here, one of their buses is seen at the former Silver End Garage after both the buses and the garage had been taken over by the Eastern National.

109 Local traders such as bakers and butchers once delivered small items by hand carts until superseded in the 1950s by light vans.

110 Although Crittall's made extensive use of the railway to transport their products, for short hauls they increasingly used motor transport. In this 1920s' picture, metal window frames are being delivered.

111   From about the turn of the century, starting in small premises in Newland Street, Glover Brothers operated one of the first garages in Witham. Here, a line of cars is seen at the corner of Collingwood Road, *c.*1910.

112   During the construction of Silver End Garden Village, *c.*1930, Crittall's made considerable use of the fledgling motor transport industry to collect gravel and sand. In this picture, gravel is being unloaded from the pit's own overhead tramway.

113 In the 1930s Joe Turner was employed as a roundsman for E.P. Palmer who ran a baker's and confectioner's shop.

114 In the late 1950s Lord Rayleigh's Dairies at Hatfield Peverel were delivering fresh milk to their customers in three ways—in bottles, in tankers and in churns.

Public Services

Schools

The first school in Witham was the National School sited next to All Saints' Church. It opened in 1842 with a roll of 100 boys, 100 girls and 90 infants. Boys and girls had separate classes. It was quickly followed in 1847 by a British School in Maldon Road. By 1952 there were three primary schools in Witham and others in Silver End and Kelvedon. National and British Schools also appeared at Hatfield Peverel and Kelvedon in the last century. In 1952 the catchment area for the Witham Secondary School covered Kelvedon, Boreham, Feering and Hatfield Peverel. Since then further schools have opened. Currently the majority are under the control of the Essex County Council.

Fire Service

Witham fire brigade progressed from a primitive horse-drawn appliance to a steam fire engine, and then the first motor vehicle was purchased in 1930 by Witham Urban District Council. After a disastrous fire towards the end of the last century, Kelvedon also established its own fire brigade, and purchased a hand pump, having raised the money by public subscription. Witham's original fire station was sited in Bridge Street next to the river Brain. During the war the service was taken over by the National Fire Service (NFS). The main station was in Guithavon Street; other appliances were stationed behind *The Swan*. After the war fire services were returned to local authority control and today the fire service is administered by the Essex Fire and Rescue Service from a combined Fire and Ambulance Station in Hatfield Road.

Post Office

Postal services in Witham and Kelvedon have a long history. At first they were very rudimentary but in 1635 King Charles I issued a proclamation making it possible for the general public to send letters along established post routes. Witham became a staging point between Brentwood and Colchester. Innkeepers were frequently appointed postmaster, and the landlord at *The George* was one of the first. Mail coaches were quite separate from stage coaches with their own livery and paid no tolls along the Great Essex turnpike.

Water

From early beginnings, when the district had to rely on wells and watercourses, the present modern system of water supply has developed. By 1952 water was supplied by the South Essex Waterworks Company from their works at Langford. Originally, there was no proper way of disposing of sewage except into cesspools and ditches, which caused obvious health hazards. However, over the years proper sewage systems gradually developed and by 1952 the Witham sewage works was situated south east of the town and the effluent was piped to discharge into the river below Langford. Today, the supply of water is the responsibility of the Essex and Suffolk Water Company and sewage disposal is the concern of Anglian Water.

Gas

Witham's gasworks was built in 1834 at a cost of £850 and was extended in 1847 with a new gasometer. The works was sited at the junction of Bridge Street with Mill Lane. Kelvedon also had its own works, conveniently located near the railway goods station, from where coal supplies were obtained. In both cases gas was made on site from coal and distributed via a series of mains leading from the works to the various consumers. The Gas Companies also installed street lamps and, as elsewhere, there were eventually replaced by electrically illuminated lamps. The works were independent until nationalised in the early 1950s by the post-war Labour Government. Manufacture of gas at both Witham and Kelvedon ceased in the 1950s, when a high pressure main was built from Chelmsford to Colchester, along the old A12, linking two modern works in those towns. North Sea Gas eventually replaced gas derived from coal. Today, the supply of gas has been returned to the private sector and the gas works site at Witham is now a car park.

115 Witham was an important postal centre during the era of mail coaches for the Braintree and Sudbury district. This continued through until 1918 when the status of the Witham office was downgraded to a sub-post office. The postmaster at Chelmsford took control of Witham and its 13 sub-offices. This group picture of the entire staff was taken outside their premises in Newland Street c.1920.

116 Witham fire brigade's first appliance, *c*.1890, was fairly primitive, consisting of a horse-drawn vehicle carrying a hand pump and a few hoses and buckets. It was operated by volunteer part-time firemen.

117 At about the same time Kelvedon also boasted its own fire brigade. They are seen here photographed here with their engine in the High Street.

118 By about 1910, the Witham fire brigade had a steam appliance, which was much more effective because of the higher velocity of the water jets. Unfortunately, the time taken to reach a fire had not improved, as the vehicle was still horse-drawn. In 1930, it was replaced by the town's first motor vehicle.

119 Since the formation of the County Police Force in 1840, Witham has had a small but effective force. The original police station, built towards the end of the 19th century in Guithavon Street, is seen here. It was replaced by the present building in Colchester Road in 1937.

120 Witham water tower in Collingwood Road, now demolished, was built to a similar distinctive design as that at Braintree, which still survives.

121 Class IV of the Board School, Maldon Road, Witham, *c.*1905. Despite the comparative poverty of the times, children were usually clean and neatly dressed. Strong parental and classroom discipline often led to excellent scholastic results.

122 Class III of the National School, Witham, *c.*1908, was an all-boys' class. The teachers at the time were (*left to right*) Mr. Smith, Mr. Cranfield and Mr. Gordie.

123 Children from the Hatfield Peverel National School pose for their picture, *c.*1905. In those days the village was still small and very rural.

124 Kelvedon School, *c.*1875, was once the largest boarding school in Essex, catering for middle-class children, particularly those whose parents were overseas. In 1851, it had 96 boarders, three teachers, four servants and a charlady. It was run by William Wiseman and was on the south side of Kelvedon Street. Its site is now occupied by the present Dominican Convent.

125 Pupils of the British School, Kelvedon, stand outside their school building with their master, John Orst, *c.*1870. Today, it is in use as the Kelvedon library.

126 The Bridge Home Hospital, Witham, *c*.1910, is at the south-western entrance of the town. It was built in 1839 as the local workhouse and features a polygonal centre block and an arched gateway. It is now under the wing of the National Health Service.

127 Collingwood Road was built in 1872 to provide direct access from the centre of Witham to the newly-built railway station. Development alongside followed, including the Public Hall, which was opened by Lord Rayleigh in 1894. This illustration is dated *c*.1910.

Recreation

128 Witham swimming pool, Bridge Street, *c.*1935. In comparison with today's heated indoor pools it offered very spartan facilities. Nevertheless, in summer it was popular for family outings and many hardy enthusiasts would turn up whatever the weather.

129 Well before modern recreational facilities were dreamt of, any suitable sheet of water was an attraction for local children, seen here enjoying a splash, *c.*1900 at Terling ford.

130 Football is an ever popular sport and in 1902-3 the Witham Football Club, photographed here before a match at The Grove, had a strong team.

131 After its founding by Baden-Powell, scouting quickly became popular and most places soon had scout groups which taught reliability, the value of team work and promoted open-air activities. The Witham Scouts are seen here on parade, *c.*1928.

The Witham Musical & Amateur Operatic Society

PRESENT

(By permission of the British Amalgamated Theatres Ltd.)

"THE MAID OF THE MOUNTAINS"

NIGHTLY AT 8 P.M.

FEB. 3 (Wed.), 4, 5 & 6.

IN THE

PUBLIC HALL, WITHAM.

POPULAR NIGHT WEDNESDAY ONLY

Reserved Seats — 2/6
Unreserved Seats — 1/-

Booking Office: Messrs. Clarke & Co., High St., Witham. Phone Witham 3.

Tickets Res. 4/6, 3/6, 2/6. Unreserved 1/6, 1/-

132 In most small towns there has always been a strong interest in amateur dramatics and Witham is no exception. In February 1937, for one week, the Witham Musical & Amateur Operatic Society staged nightly their version of *The Maid of the Mountains* at the Public Hall.

133 As part of the creation of a garden village at Silver End in the early 1930s, the Development Company also created leisure facilities, including a recreation ground. The Memorial Gardens are seen here about 1955.

WHITEHALL – WITHAM
PHONE 142

WEEK COMMENCING SUNDAY, JANUARY 11th, at 5.30 p.m.
HUGHIE GREEN & MARGARET LOCKWOOD in MELODY & ROMANCE
and Full Supporting Programme

MONDAY, TUESDAY & WEDNESDAY, continuous from 5 p.m
VIRGINIA BRUCE & DENNIS MORGAN in
FLIGHT ANGELS
With **Wayne Morris** and **Ralph Bellamy**
Also *JAMES STEPHENSON* in
CALLING PHILO VANCE

THURS., FRI. & SAT., continuous from   Saturday Matinee at 2 o'clock
Diana Winyard and Michael Redgrave in
KIPPS
AND FULL SUPPORTING PROGRAMME

134 Before television, most people went to the movies at least once a week. For many years Witham's only cinema was the Whitehall. Originally built as a private house, it became a cinema after the First World War and is shown here about 1935. It closed in the 1970s and is now the Witham library.

135 Reproduced here is the programme for the week commencing 11 January 1942.

136 Witham Recreation Ground, *c*.1910. It was opened to the public on 20 June 1900, though it remained in the ownership of Percy Lawrence of The Grove until 1903.

Wartime

137 During the First World War substantial numbers of soldiers were stationed in the area as part of a strategic reserve held against any surprise invasion by the enemy. At Witham, in addition to the soldiers, there was also a Red Cross Hospital. On parade in this picture are some nurses together with some of their charges. The hospital closed in 1919.

138 *(top right)*   With large numbers of young nurses and soldiers thrown together in a small town, it was perhaps inevitable that romance would blossom. This card was sent by a soldier to his sister in Birmingham.

139 *(bottom right)*   Near The Avenue, during the First World War, the army had a temporary camp. Horses were used in large numbers to pull wagons and artillery as well as providing cavalry mounts. Here, the local blacksmith is shoeing one of the horses.

The R.A.M.C. are "holding their own" at WITHAM.

140 In both World Wars the majority of young men throughout Britain either volunteered or were conscripted into the Armed Forces. In the First World War casualties were particularly heavy and few families were left untouched. The Witham war memorial was unveiled on 20 November 1920.

141 In 1939 elaborate preparations for civil defence were made, once war seemed inevitable. Air Raid Wardens and Special Policemen were recruited, given basic training and issued with tin helmets and gas masks. In 1939, the Witham force posed for this group picture.

142 Although Witham was not a prime target for enemy raiders, it did suffer some bomb damage. Luckily the first bomb landed in open farm land and the explosion was absorbed by the soft ground. The army quickly examined the ensuing crater.

143 In 1941 Crittall's factory received a direct hit and suffered considerable damage. However, the factory recovered and went on to make a substantial contribution to the war effort.

144 A group picture of the members of the Kelvedon post of the Royal Observer Corps on 23 June 1940. The Corps was not finally stood down until after the end of the Cold War.

145 With the entry of America into the Second World War, scores of military airfields were constructed on first-class agricultural land throughout Essex and East Anglia, including one at Rivenhall. From here many bombing missions were undertaken over occupied Europe. Later, it was a station for gliders taking part in air drops over Belgium and Holland.

146 The inside of one of the temporary Nissen huts which provided accommodation for the air crews in 1944.

397th
BOMB GROUP

147 This dramatic picture, taken on H-hour D-day 1944, shows a USAAF Marauder bomber of 397 Bomb Group sharply etched against the night sky.

148 The crew and maintenance engineers stand proudly beside their plane, the Leaping Lena, the veteran of over 40 bombing missions from Rivenhall, 1944.

149 Also at the airfield were men of the 597 Communications Section. Some are seen here displaying a collection of cameras used in photographing enemy targets.

150 Even in the war GIs needed a break for their coffee and doughnuts. At Rivenhall these were served from a mobile canteen donated by the people of North Carolina.

151 After the liberation of France, the 397 Bomb Group USAAF moved to France and were replaced at Rivenhall by 295 Squadron 38 Group RAF, who flew Short Sterling bombers. One of their duties was towing Horsa gliders, which took part in various air drops, October 1944.

152 Horsa gliders parked on the main runway at Rivenhall Airfield, 7 October 1944.

153 During the war, conscription of most able-bodied men resulted in a shortage of labour down on the farm and the Women's Land Army was formed to overcome this. They took on many jobs previously undertaken by men. Here a girl at Lord Rayleigh's Taylors Farm, *c.*1944, leads Terling Torch to the milking parlour. This Friesian won many championships and, when pictured, was 16 years old and had just produced her 13th calf.

154 Here the same Land Army girl is seen breaking cattle cake for the herd. Interestingly, the grinder was made locally by the now defunct firm of Bentall & Co. of Heybridge. In 1944 it was one of the best-known manufacturers of agricultural machinery.

Events

WRECK OF THE CROMER EXPRESS, G.E.R. AT WITHAM. Sep.1st. 1905.

No 640
Fred Spalding
photo.
Chelmsford.
Copyright.

155, 156 & 157   One of the most dramatic railway accidents took place at Witham station in September 1905, when the Cromer Express left the track. Several of the flimsy wooden carriages disintegrated, with debris scattered across the platforms. Among those who photographed the disaster was Fred Spalding, the well-known Chelmsford photographer, who took these pictures.

WRECK OF THE CROMER EXPRESS. G.E.R. AT WITHAM. Sep. 1st 1905.

Fred Spalding
Photo
Chelmsford
Copyright

No 641.

158 The Essex Agricultural Show, until after the Second World War, was moved each year to a different venue. In 1910 it was held at The Avenue fields and was enthusiastically received by the townspeople. Today, the show is permanently sited at Great Leighs but its long-term future is in some doubt.

159 The meet of the local hunt outside the *White Hart* in Newland Street at the turn of the century.

160 The opening of Witham swimming pool by Valentine Crittall, *c.*1930, was attended by councillors from the Witham Urban District and various local dignitaries. The Crittall Manufacturing Company Ltd. was a substantial benefactor to both Witham and Silver End.

161 The annual 'gathering in' of the harvest has always been a cause for celebration both in church and on the farm. This picture was taken at Terling *c.*1900, showing employees of Lord Rayleigh's Farms enjoying a formal harvest supper.

162 & 163 The funeral of Admiral Sir W.G. Luard KCB on 24 May 1910 was an impressive affair, with the funeral cortège preceded by a brass band and followed by a long procession of horse-drawn carriages passing down Newland Street. He died at the age of 90, the result of an accident when he was thrown from his carriage when it collided with a telegraph pole.

164 The Boer War was a hard-fought conflict, with the British, despite superior numbers, suffering many reverses. The relief in 1900 of the besieged and starving garrison at Mafeking was greeted throughout the country with patriotic fervour. The main streets of Witham were decorated with bunting and the townspeople gathered to watch a procession through the town.

165 Even today, the old timber-framed buildings in Newland Street present a fire hazard. On 9 February 1910, the Constitutional Club and Institute caught fire and the Witham Fire Brigade could do little except prevent the fire from engulfing the adjacent properties. It was never rebuilt and today remains as an open area in front of the present United Reform Church.

166 The Hollies at Kelvedon is seen here decorated with bunting and patriotic slogans at the time of King Edward VII's Coronation in 1902.

167 On 30 October 1940, a 500lb bomb exploded next to the Old Rectory, Terling, creating a massive crater, smashing all the windows in the house and removing the roof. Luckily no one was seriously hurt. This picture was taken a few days afterwards when temporary repairs had been carried out.

Witham Co-operative Society, Limited

Registered Office and Central Premises: High Street, Witham.

" The old order changeth, yielding place to new."

New Shopping Facilities

FOR

Hatfield Peverel Residents

WHERE

QUALITY IS TIP-TOP AND DIVIDEND IS MOST WELCOME

The new Branch Store of the Witham Co-operative Society, Limited, situate at the Green, Hatfield Peverel, consisting of

GROCERY & PROVISIONS, DRAPERY, CLOTHING, OUTFITTING, BOOTS & SHOES, HARDWARE, &c.

will be Officially Opened at 3 p.m. on

Saturday, October 22nd, 1932
by **Mr. T. W. Johnson,**

(President of the Society).

168 In October 1932, the Witham Co-operative Society's new branch shop at The Green, Hatfield Peverel was proudly opened by their President, Mr. T.W. Johnson.

People

169 One of Witham's most famous sons was Admiral Sir William Garnham Luard KCB. On retirement from the navy he became active in town affairs, and is seen here addressing a large crowd who, in 1905, commemorated the centenary of the Battle of Trafalgar and the death of Nelson.

170 It was through Francis Crittall's vision that Silver End was developed as a pioneer garden village. He was one of the first people to move there, living in 'The Manors' from 1927 until his death in 1935. He is seen here with his wife, Ellen.

171 The Hon. Edward Strutt (1859-1930) took over the family estate at Terling and developed Lord Rayleigh's Farms. During the First World War he was Chief Agricultural Adviser to the Ministry of Agriculture.

172 Dr. Varenne was a popular Kelvedon doctor, with a substantial practice. He was also an expert in botanical studies, as well as being the Secretary of the local Liberal Association. He died in 1887 aged 77.

173 Inspector Richard Giggins and his men at Witham Police Station, 1939. Those in the rear row are equipped with the wartime standard tin helmet and service respirator in case of gas attack.

Bibliography

Benham, Hervey, *Some Essex Water Mills* (1976)
Booker, John, *Essex and the Industrial Revolution* (1974)
Brake, David, *Window Vision* (1989)
Crawley, R.J. *et al*, *The Years Between*, vols.1 and 2 (1984)
Crittall, Francis, *Fifty Years of Work and Play* (1935)
Essex Records Office, *Railways in Essex (until 1923)* (1978)
Gavin, Sir William, *Ninety Years of Family Farming* (1967)
Gifford, P.R., *Witham in Old Postcards* (1980)
Jarvis, Stan, *The Rivers Chelmer and Blackwater* (1990)
Kelvedon Parish Council, *Kelvedon Footpaths & Bridleways* (1994)
Lord Rayleigh's and Strutt & Parker Farms (1994)
Marriage, John, *Braintree and Bocking: A Pictorial History* (1994)
Marriage, John, *Changing Chelmsford* (1992)
Mead, F.J., *Silver End* (unpublished thesis)
Moores of Kelvedon, ECC leaflet (1993)
Palombi, John, *Witham & District* (1995)
Paye, Peter, *The Tollesbury Branch* (1985)
Pevsner, Nikolaus, *The Buildings of England: Essex* (1954)
Scarfe, Norman, *Essex* (1978)
Scollan, Maureen, *Fifty Years of Silver End* (1975)
Smith, M.L., *Early History of Witham* (1970)
Smith, M.L., *Fires in Witham* (1975)
Smith, M.L., *Postal History of Witham* (1971)
Swindale, D.L., *Branch Lines to Maldon* (1977)
Thornton, D., *Just the Ticket* (1980)
White, William, *History of the County of Essex* (1848)
Witham & Countryside Society, *Guide to Chipping Hill*
Witham & Countryside Society, *Guide to Newland Street, Witham*
Witham—Official Guide (1994)
Women's Institute, *Essex Town & Country* (1992)

Various issues of: *Witham and Braintree Times*, *Essex Chronicle*, *Essex County Standard* and *Essex Countryside*.

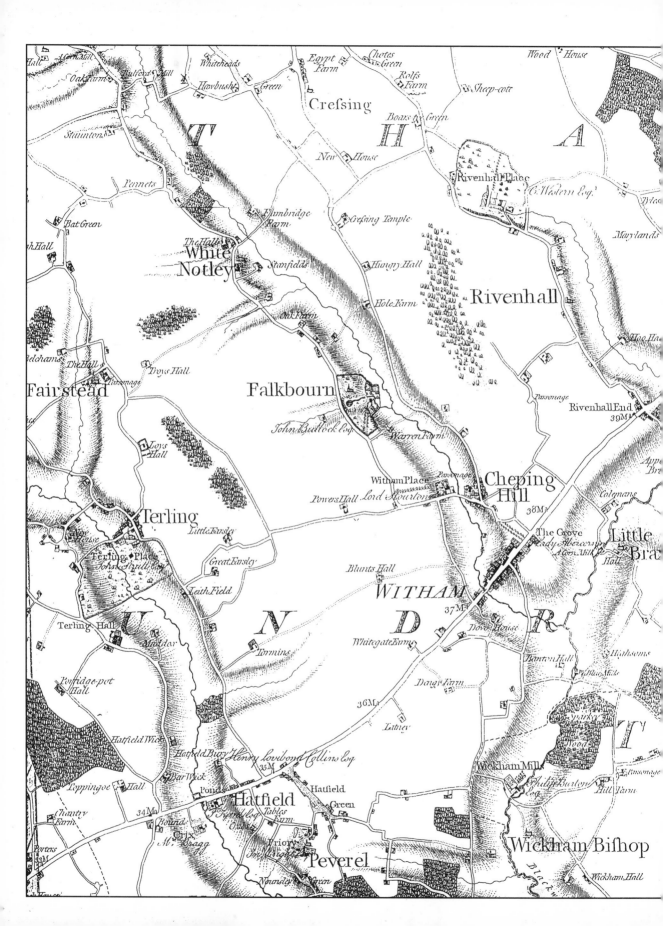